© 1992 Franklin Watts

Franklin Watts
96 Leonard Street
London
EC2A 4RH

Franklin Watts Inc,
387 Park Avenue South
New York, NY 10016

Franklin Watts Australia
14 Mars Road
Lane Cove
NSW 2066

UK ISBN: 0 7496 0783 1

A CIP catalogue record for this book is available
from the British Library.

Editor: Sarah Ridley
Designer: Janet Watson
Illustrator: Linda Costello

Photographs: Eye Ubiquitous 7; Chris Fairclough
Colour Library 9, 10, 14, 19; Robert Harding
Picture Library front cover, 23, 25; Hutchison
Library 26; Thames Water Plc 17, 20; ZEFA title
page, 13.

Printed in Singapore.

LIFT OFF!

THE WATER CYCLE

Joy Richardson

FRANKLIN WATTS
London • New York • Sydney • Toronto

Water everywhere

Three-quarters of the earth
is covered with water.

Plants, animals and people
are all made mostly of water.
Every living thing needs
water to survive.

Water is the most ordinary
thing in the world and
the most extraordinary.

Changing water

Water can change its form.
It is not always a liquid.

It can freeze into solid ice
which is lighter than water
and takes up more space.

It can dry up into the air
and become an invisible gas
called water vapour.

Water vapour

Water can turn into water vapour
and back into water again.
This is how rain is made.

Water dries up from the surface of
oceans and seas, rivers and reservoirs.
Puddles disappear and the ground dries out.

All this drying up is called evaporation.
The water has not been lost.
It has turned into water vapour in the air.

Making clouds

Warm air carries the water vapour
up into the sky where it cools down.

If the air is loaded with water vapour,
tiny water droplets begin to form.
This is called condensation.

The water droplets make clouds.
The drops join up and grow bigger
as they sink to the bottom of the cloud.

Heavy raindrops fall out.

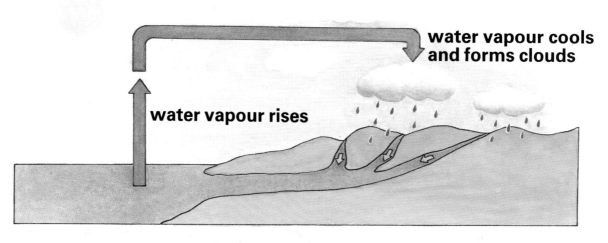

water vapour cools
and forms clouds

water vapour rises

Rainwater

Rain provides the water
we use in our homes.

Rainwater soaks down
into underground rocks.
It flows into rivers and
is collected in reservoirs.

It can be pumped out when
it is needed.

It flows through pipes to the
treatment works to be cleaned.

Ready for use

At the treatment works,
the water is filtered.
It soaks through beds of sand
which catch the dirt and germs.

Chemicals are added to make
the water safe to drink.

The clean water is pumped into
storage tanks or water towers.

It is ready to be used.

Out of the tap

Clean water flows through
pipes to your house.
When you turn on a tap,
it comes rushing out.

We use a lot of water
for cooking and drinking,
washing and cleaning.

Dirty water runs away
down the plughole but that
is not the end of the story.

Cleaning water

Used water runs through pipes to the sewage works where it is strained and cleaned.

Then it can be pumped back into rivers or into the sea.

If the water is well cleaned, the same water may be used again and again.

Rivers

When rain falls on the land,
some of it trickles
into ditches and streams.

Streams flow downhill
and join up into rivers.

Rivers flow down to the sea
and pour out all the water
they have collected on the way.

Salt water

River water picks up traces of salt
from rocks in the river bed
as it washes over them.

The salt mixes with the water
which flows into the sea.
The sea is too salty to drink.

When water evaporates from the sea,
it leaves its salt behind.

Fresh rainwater falls on the land.
It can be used for drinking.

Underground water

Some parts of the world
have very little rain.

In these places, water is difficult to find
and it is very precious.

There may be water hidden
deep under the ground.
If springs and wells
bring it to the surface,
even the desert can blossom.

Water cycle

More than half of you is water.
You take in water from
your food and drink.
You lose water when you sweat.

Plants suck up water from the ground
and let it out through their leaves.

All living things are
part of the water cycle
which keeps the world alive.

Index

Air 8, 11, 12

Clouds 12
Condensation 12

Desert 27

Evaporation 11, 24

Gas 8

Ice 8

Land 22, 24
Liquid 8

Pipes 15, 18, 21
Plants 6, 28

Rain 11, 15, 22, 27

Raindrops 12
Rainwater 15, 24
Reservoirs 11, 15
Rivers 11, 15, 21, 22, 24
Rocks 15, 24

Salt 24
Seas 11, 21, 22, 24
Sewage works 21
Springs 27
Streams 22

Tap 18
Treatment works 15, 16

Water cycle 28
Water towers 16
Water vapour 8, 11, 12
Wells 27